Positive Thoughts

for a

Profitable Day

James Scott Bernard

Bernard Publishing

Warrenton, Oregon 97146

ISBN 978-0-9961665-8-4

This book is meant to be an encouragement to you and is dedicated to and for all we humans who seek to encourage ourselves and others.

Contents

Winning

How do you get and keep that winning feeling?

Work at a pace that makes you win. Have lots of little victories every day.

In between wins, do within when you're doing without. Focus on past wins.

Never stop, never give up!

6 E's for Success

#1 Expectancy, expect the best.

#2 Expand your horizons.

#3 Explore new areas of service.

#4 Exercise your total talents.

#5 Experience the joy and meaning
   of each moment.

#6 Excitement is all that you do.
   Exude enthusiasm.

Action

Here's the action formula for success!

Act. Nothing happens until you act!

Consistent action brings consistent results.

Timeliness. Today not tomorrow.

Indecision is a Decision

One thing at a time, the key to overcoming obstacles.

Never give up, new ideas, new direction, never give up!

Boldness

A key characteristic of the successful is: Boldness, and what is the basis of our Boldness? From the New Testament: "For God has not given us a Spirit of Timidity but of power, love and a sound mind," And from the Old Testament: "But the righteous are Bold as a lion." When we're doing it right we can be Bold as a lion!

Maintaining a Positive Attitude

How do you maintain a Positive Attitude?

Two keys:

First, be a Positive Perceiver and what's a Positive Perceiver? Someone who looks for (perceives), the best in any situation or person.

Second, be a Positive Purveyor and what's a Positive Purveyor? Someone who gives (purveys) their best in any situation.

Making Success a Habit

Success is a habit! Force yourself to follow the Principles of Success long enough for them to become a habit and success for you is assured. Many of us cheat ourselves by not following the Principles of Success long enough for them to become a habit, a part of us. Habit can help us, or hinder us, harness it and make it your helper!

Resiliency

A key characteristic of the successful is:

Resiliency: and what is resiliency?

1) It's being flexible enough to try something new.

2) Flexible enough to risk failure and

3) Resiliency is the ability to bounce back and keep trying!

The 4 Ds for Success

1) Have a DREAM.

2) Have DESIRE enough to do something about it.

3) DECIDE to get started.

4) DETERMINATION, the guts to stick with it, to keep going!

6 Words for Success

They say the 6 Key Words for success are these:

FIND A NEED AND FILL IT
and what are man's greatest needs?

"A desire to feel important, to be accepted, help others and yourself to feel important, to be accepted and you're on your way to success."

Gracefulness

Gracefulness has been defined to be the outward expression of the inward harmony of the soul, a graceful person is:

Genial, Gentle, a Go-giver.

Respects the rights of others, refusing to get ruffled and riled.

Allows for the imperfections of self and others.

Caring, calm, cool, collected, and composed.

Embraces life with all its verities and empathy, expectations, and enthusiasm.

Looking for Possibilities

Successful people look for possibilities in three areas:

1) Possibilities within themselves, most of us are realizing only about 10% of our potential.
2) Possibilities in the situation look for the promise in the problem.

3) Possibilities in others. Instead of putting people down, pray them up!

Truth

Emerson said: "The greatest homage we can pay to truth is to use it."

And what is truth?

Tell it like it is.
Recognize reality; see things for what they really are.
Understanding heart.
Think things through: i.e. what's going to be the results of my present actions?
Have the heart to act on the truth you have.

Peace

A prescription for personal peace:

Practice patience with yourself and others.

Easy flowingness with life.

Accept all that comes your way as an opportunity for growth.

Courage, call up the courage to become all you can be.

Embrace all of life in a spirit of positive expectancy.

Problems

When faced with a problem

1) Don't panic.

2) Pause.

3) Place your mind is neutral.

4) Puncture pressure.

5) Proceed with possible solutions.

ESP Formula

Here's a simple ESP formula for optimism:

Expose your mind to positive uplifting thoughts.

Self talk—make it Positive and Supportive.

Picture in your mind the Positive outcome of a Predetermined Plan.

Desire

A Key ingredient for Success is Desire.

And what is Desire?

Define and decide what you want.

Eliminate conflicting elements.

Set definite goals.

Initiate immediate action.

Release and regiment all resources for it realization.

Expect, Experience and enjoy an excellent ending.

A Blaze of Success

A fireplace fire is sputtering about to go out and you rearrange the pieces, add a little kindling and you have a Blazing Inferno. The same is true in our lives. Things can be down to what seems to be the last little "puff" of smoke, rearrange your priorities, add a little kindling of faith and initiative and the little "puff" of smoke turns into a "Blaze of Success."

The ABCs of Self Esteem

Appreciate, affirm and acclaim your own uniqueness.

Be your own Best Friend—from beginning to end.

Call forth the courage to become all you were intended to become.

Getting on with Our Lives

On several occasions while drift fishing on Oregon streams, our boat would slip into an "eddy" out of the main stream and unless extra effort in rowing took place the boat would remain trapped in the eddy, the "circular" motion of the water.

Many of our lives get trapped in an "eddy" of circumstances or habit that keeps us from moving on in the main stream of life. We need to take the Oars of Thought and Action, redefining and reaffirming our short and long term goals and move on into the main stream of our futures.

The Seeds of Success

Each one of us has built within us; it comes as standard equipment, a Success Mechanism, the Seeds for Success. What is this Success Mechanism and how does it work? It's the deep desire within each one of us to feel important, to amount to something, to make a difference.

How do we activate our success mechanism?

1) By not ignoring the desire to feel important.
2) Pursue to the ultimate the areas of your greatest interest.
3) Recognize that you have untapped potential.
4) Begin now!

Divinely Designed Discontent

I guess that we all get the feeling from time to time as the lyrics of the song go: "Is that all there is?" A feeling that we're not enough or that we're not experiencing or realizing all that we were intended to experience, that there must be more to life than what we're experiencing. Could it be that this feeling of discontent is our creators Divinely Designed Plan to encourage us to experience and become all that we were created to be? Let that feeling of discontent motivate and encourage you and drive you in the direction of your dreams.

Happiness

If we were to put happiness under the magnifying glass of careful scrutiny, I think we'd find that it results from "Right" relationship: Right relationships with "ourselves," with "others" and with our "God."

A Formula for Happiness

From Micah 6:8

"He has shown you o' man what is good and what does the Lord require of you? But to do justly, to love mercy, and to walk humbly with your God."

When we do justly, we feel good about ourselves. When we show mercy, we cut a little slack for others and ourselves. And when we walk humbly with our God, we seek to "toot" the other person's horn rather than our own.

Possibilities

We all face problems. So how do we handle them? The secret is not to find victory over our problems, but to find victory in our problems. Look for the possibilities, the promise in the problem.

Dreams

Have you got a Dream? If not, why not? "Cause how ya gonna have a dream come true if you don't have a Dream?" Don't kill your Dream. Execute it!

3 Keys to Happiness

1) Happiness is a Decision: Abraham Lincoln said, "Most people are about as happy as they make up their mind to be."

2) Happiness is "Within"—even Jesus said, "The Kingdom of Heaven is within."

3) Happiness is losing ourselves in something bigger than ourselves!

Change

One of the greatest blessings, greatest hopes for any of us is that because of the "Plasticity" of our nature we have the ability to change. If we have learned negative, unprofitable behavior, we can unlearn it! Hallelujah! We can change! Can a leopard change its spots? Probably not, BUT WE CAN CHANGE!

Anger

A prescription for anger:

Always put time between yourself and the aggravating solution.

Neutralize anger by not buying into it in the first place.

Give a fair appraisal of the adversaries' position.

Explore areas of agreement and positive resolution.

Refuse to let the situation control you.

Persistence

Here is a special message In Persistence from: a Light Bulb, a Whiskey Bottle, and a Clam Shell:

First, a Light Bulb: Thomas Edison failed over 4,000 times before he perfected the light bulb. He persisted.

Second, a Whiskey Bottle: The Cyrus Noble mine was sold for a bottle of whiskey. The new owner found one of the richest veins of gold only inches from where the previous owner quit. He failed to persist!

Third, a Clam Shell: On a trip to the Oregon Coast clam digging, I was experiencing very poor results. I would spot the small oval in the sand where I was certain there would be a clam, dig with great "fury," but no clam Finally, I thought maybe I'm not digging deep enough. Sure enough, by digging just a few inches deeper—Bingo! A clam every time! Important point: It takes almost as much effort to almost get a clam as it does to get one. It takes almost as much effort to almost succeed as it does to succeed!

Abundance Attitude

Instead of focusing upon what you lack, focus upon what you have, count your blessings! It gives you a Plus Platform to build from. Even Jesus, finding himself on a mountainside with 5,000 hungry people said to his disciples: What have we got to work with?" Five loaves and two fish and what did he do? He blessed it! He gave thanks for what he had and it multiplied. Give thanks for what you have and watch it multiply—it's almost like magic!

What about lack and tough situations? In Ephesians 5:20 we're told: Giving thanks always for all things." Here's the real secret! Look at what you "lack" as the great opportunity of Growth! Hey! I haven't arrived yet! The trips not over! I've still got lots of Ports of Call to go, new areas to develop and explore! Thanks God! There's always more to know, a place to go! An opportunity to grow!

Pinning Medals on Yourself

A real key to high self esteem is: not waiting for others to pin medals on you, but pinning medals on yourself!

If you're always looking for or waiting for the approval and recognition of others, you may have a long wait and ultimately be disappointed.

The secret is to pin your own medals on, be a success in your own eyes, give yourself credit for a job well done, for an accomplishment.

Highest and Best Use

In Real Estate Development, the true test for the property's use is: "What is the highest and best use of a Particular Property?" Often Property suited for a much higher use is developed for lower uses. For example, waterfront property is developed for parking rather than a High-Rise Condo. The same can be true in our lives. Are we making "The Highest and Best" use of our lives or have we settled for less than our best?

9 Keys to Happiness

Help others get what they want and happiness happens!

Always give more than you get. (A positive personal balance sheet and you'll never be overdrawn in personal relationships.)

Push, Plot, Pilot, Pluck your path to your Platform of Total Potential.

Put yourself in the other person's place.

Investigate new areas of interest.

Negate all negativism.

Expect the best in each and every event.

Set and stick to success standards.

Savor, Sanctify, and Salvage each second.

Positive Self Expectancy

Expect Success

X—multiply your talent by using it! (What you don't use, you lose.)

Plan, Prepare, and Practice the success you expect.

Educare (Latin for educate) to call forth the giant from within.

Clarify your expectations.

Think tall thoughts which is: Picturing in your mind the positive outcome of a Predetermined Plan.

Having a Great Day

We often hear the comment, "Have a good day!" "Have a Great Day!" I, like many, have pondered what really makes for a "Great Day" and is it possible to make every day a Great Day? For me at least it starts with a hearty and grateful respect for the gift of life with all its verities. The Psalmist expressed it this way: "So teach us to number our days that we might apply our hearts unto Wisdom." It's being aware of all the wonders that are occurring about us and within us. Developing a "Serendipitous Expectancy;" i.e. looking for the happy surprises all around us; a bird singing, a pussy willow heralding the approach of spring, the taste of real maple syrup, the inner feeling of satisfaction from a job well done. It's appreciating the true uniqueness of all our fellow sojourners as well as our own uniqueness. It's being flexible and responsive to changing environments and situations. It's seeking the seed for growth and opportunity in even the most obtrusive situation.

Having a great day, every day, results from filling each day with the ingredients for a great day:

1) Positive thoughts.
2) Proper exercise and diet.
3) Meditation and study.
4) Goal setting and review.
5) Total commitment in your chosen line of endeavor.
6) Recreation.
7) Sufficient rest.

If each day includes these ingredients, we can predict all our future days and they will be "Great Days!"

Time Toughness

One thing that all we humans have in common is twenty-four hours of time each day. Be we old or young, rich or poor, we all have the same amount of time each day.

How we spend that time will determine not only our present, but our future. Time is like a "conveyor-belt"—it continues to run whether we put anything on it or not.

Ask yourself this question: "Am I making the very best use of my time right now?" *and* "Where will I be in three years from today if I continue to spend my time in the same manner?" Got any special plans, goals, or dreams? Set them in motion, get started! Do it now!

About the Author

At the age of sixteen Jim Bernard crossed the Columbia River Bar as an ordinary seaman. He received his Deck Officer's license at twenty-one and served during the Korean War.

In college, Jim majored in business, psychology, and religion.

After leaving the sea Jim went on to build an insurance and real estate business in Portland, Oregon. After selling the business, Jim and Cherie moved to Astoria, Oregon where Jim assisted in the management of a Ford dealership.

Jim and Cherie charter fished out of Hammond, Oregon. Jim, until recently, served as a captain and guide at Yes Bay, Alaska taking guests fishing for salmon, halibut and other bottom fish.

Jim served as an elder and teaches in the Presbyterian Church.

Jim and Cherie live in Warrenton, Oregon, less than a mile from the Mighty Columbia River. They are proud parents of four children, fourteen grandchildren, and twenty great-grandchildren. They have been happily married for sixty-six years and have always been blessed by a living and loving Lord.

Books by the Author

Alaska Fishing Adventures (2015)

Inspirational Nautical Poems and Prose (2015)

Making the Principles of Success a Habit

Positive Poems and Rhymes (2015)

Positive Thoughts for a Profitable Day (2015)

The Adventures of a Young Merchant Sailor (2015)

www.ingramcontent.com/pod-product-compliance
Lightning Source LLC
Chambersburg PA
CBHW051713090426
42736CB00013B/2684